Trees of the Caribbean

S. A. Seddon and G. W. Lennox

CARIBBEAN

First published 1980 by
MACMILLAN EDUCATION LTD
London and Oxford
Companies and representatives throughout the world

ISBN 0–333–28793–2

19   18   17   16   15   14   13   12   11
07   06   05   04   03   02   01   00   99

This book is printed on paper suitable for recycling and
made from fully managed and sustained forest sources.

Printed in Hong Kong

All the photographs are courtesy of the authors except
Norfolk Islands Pine which is by courtesy of M. Bourne.

Front cover *Poinciana (Delonix regia)*
Back cover *Pheonix canariensis*

Contents

Introduction

Part 1   Ornamental Trees

African Tulip 2
Baobab 3
Bauhinia 4
Bearded Fig 5
Bottle Brush 6
Calabash 8
Cannonball 10
Crepe Myrtle 12
Divi-Livi 13
Frangipani 14
Indian Almond 15
Indian Banyan 16
Lignum Vitae 17
Indian Laburnum 19

Mahoe 20
Norfolk Island Pine 21
Pink Cassia 23
Pink Poui 25
Poinciana 26
Pride of Burma 27
Pride of India 28
Rubber 29
Silk Cotton 30
Soufrière 31
Tamarind 32
Yellow Elder 33
Yellow Poui 35

Part 2   Fruit Trees

Akee 39
Avocado 41
Banana 43
Breadfruit 44
Cashew 45
Cocoa 47

Jack Fruit 49
Mango 50
Nutmeg 51
Pawpaw 53
Sapodilla 54
Soursop 55

Part 3   Coast Trees

Casuarina 58
Manchineel 59

Cordia 61
Sea Grape 63

Part 4   Palms and Palm-Like Trees

Cabbage Palm 66
Coconut Palm 67
Cycad 68

Royal Palm 69
Traveller's Tree 70
Screw Pine 71

Introduction

This book has been written as a companion to *Flowers of the Caribbean,* by the same authors. Inevitably, there must be some overlap between the two books but, in this volume, the authors have limited their writing and attempted to help the casual visitor or tourist to the Caribbean identify only the more common and interesting trees likely to be encountered during a short stay in the islands.

The text is divided into four main areas: Ornamental Trees, Fruit Trees, Coastal Trees and Palms and Palm-like forms. Each species is illustrated with at least one colour photograph (in many cases more than one is used) and detailed information is given about leaf shape, leaf size and colour, together with descriptions of the specific flowers and fruits. In addition, information regarding flowering times is included but, to some extent, this varies from island to island and it is not always possible to be precise.

The text is written so that little or no botanical training is required in order to make accurate identifications of the various species of tree encountered but, should the reader wish to study particular species in more detail, the botanical family name is given together with the relevant scientific name. Thus, the more serious reader has a starting point when beginning to consult more advanced texts.

Although the more common and spectacular species have been illustrated and described, other types, less common, but of considerable botanical or historical interest have also been included. For example, the Soufrière Tree (*Spachea perforata*) in the Botanical Gardens in St. Vincent is described because it is one of only three known specimens in existence and is, therefore, of considerable botanical interest. Other species not particularly common in their distribution are described, mainly because of the spectacular nature of their blossoms. The Pride of Burma (*Amherstia nobiles*) is rare. Two specimens grow in and near Port of Spain, Trinidad, and the tree is also found in Hope Gardens in Jamaica and the Botanical Gardens in Dominica. Despite its rarity, however, its inclusion in this book is justified on the grounds that it is considered by many to be the finest of all tropical flowering trees.

All the species included in this book were photographed in the Caribbean by the authors, whose sincere hope it is that the reader will derive as much pleasure as they do from observing the natural beauty and colour of these trees.

1 Ornamental Trees

Pink Poui (*Tabebuia pentaphylla*)

Family Bignoniaceae

African Tulip (*Spathodea campanulata*)
Other names Flame of the Forest, Fountain Tree, Tulipan

This large tree often attains a height of forty or fifty feet. First discovered in West Africa in the late eighteenth century, it has since been introduced into many tropical countries. The leaves are large and compound and each leaf has four to eight pairs of elliptical leaflets. The flowers are red with some yellow and they grow in circular formations, often in greater numbers towards the top of the tree. After flowering, the tree produces large boat-shaped pods, each one measuring between one and two feet. The tree flowers sporadically throughout the year in many islands but it also has peak flowering times; in Barbados it is at its best between September and late May whereas in Jamaica, which is further north, it blooms most effectively between January and May. The specimen photographed here grows in the grounds of the Paradise Beach Hotel, Barbados.

Family Bombacaceae

Baobab (*Adansonia digitata*)
Other names Bottle Tree, Monkey-Bread

This tree originated in Africa and is a common feature of some of the dry
savannas of East Africa. It is easily recognised by its huge trunk, sometimes measuring as much as thirty feet in diameter. The trunk stores water.
The tree produces pendant white flowers from which develop large woody
fruits; the latter are easily seen when the leaves drop off after flowering has
finished. It is a rare tree in the Caribbean, but two particularly fine specimens can be seen on Barbados, perhaps the best being the one in Queen's
Park, Bridgetown. It is this one which appears in this photograph.

Family Leguminoseae

Bauhinia (*Bauhinia purpurea*)
Other names Orchid Tree, Butterfly Tree, Bull Hoof Tree

This is a small tree reaching a height of between fifteen and twenty feet. It produces a spreading crown from a short thick trunk. The tree originated in India and South East Asia but has now been introduced into many Caribbean islands including Barbados and St. Vincent. The leaves have the characteristic shape of a 'cloven hoof'. Each leaf is bilobed, each lobe being about three inches long and two inches wide. The flowers are large with exposed male and female parts; in some respects they resemble the floral structures of orchids, hence the common name. Flowering takes place between October and February. The fruit bodies are flat, brown pods each about eight inches long. The specimen illustrated was photographed in St. Vincent.

Family Moraceae

Bearded Fig (*Ficus citrifolia*)

The first Portuguese explorers noticed large numbers of these fig trees when they arrived in Barbados in the sixteenth century. The trees produce heavy growths of fine hanging roots and the Portuguese gave them the name *Las Barbudas*, a translation of which means 'the bearded ones'. Some historians suggest that this is the origin of the present-day name of the island. After the first English settlers arrived in Barbados in the early 1600's the island gradually became deforested as agriculture developed and, as a result, many of the native forests of Bearded Fig disappeared. However, specimens can still be seen on the island today and there are particularly good examples in the Andromeda Gardens and also Welchman Hall Gully. This photograph is of the specimen in Andromeda Gardens.

Bottle Brush (*Callistemom lanceolatus*)

This tree, which originated in Australia, grows to a height of about twenty feet. It is not found everywhere in the Caribbean but its striking and unusual flowers make it worth including in this text. The unusual spiky appearance of each bloom results from the large number of red stamens and this arrangement results in a floral structure which resembles a brush used for cleaning babies' bottles, hence the common name. The foliage is light green in colour and the leaves are narrow and pointed.

Family   Bignoniaceae

Calabash (*Crescentia cujete*)

This tree grows to a height of about thirty feet. The branches are long and form a spreading habit. The characteristic arrangement of the leaves is in clustered or condensed spirals on reduced shoots borne on long thin branches. The habit is strangely gaunt and the clusters of leaves are themselves spiraly arranged on the branches. Each leaf is between two and five inches long. The texture is leathery and the colour is bright green on the upper surface and paler below. The flowers are bell-shaped, each about two inches with a pale yellow colour. The flowers are pollinated by nocturnal, nectar-sipping bats which find the floral structures by echolocation. The fruits are globular in shape and large specimens may grow to more than twelve inches in diameter. The central pulp and seeds are often removed, leaving a hard woody shell; such structures are watertight and are frequently used for holding water (they are called Gourds) and they are also used as ornaments. The Calabash is a native of the Caribbean and tropical America.

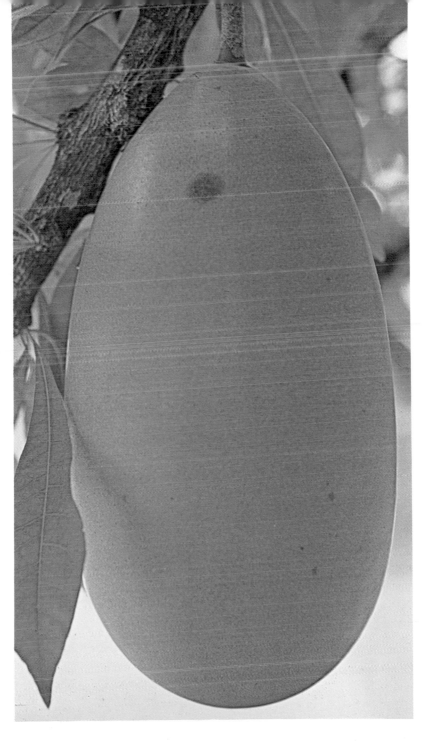

Cannonball (*Couroupita guianensis*)
Other names   Carrion Tree

This is a rare tree in most Caribbean islands. It originated in South America and has been introduced into the Caribbean as an ornamental tree. The tree reaches a height of fifty feet. The leaves are large and elliptical, each being about a foot long and four inches wide. The flowers and fruits are found on the lower part of the tree. They are borne on a mass of dangling, thin, crooked branches. Each flower is a dull red and yellowish-white in colour with a diameter of about five inches. The flowers produce a sweet smelling odour and it is suggested that their 'saucer shape' attracts pollinating agents such as bats. The tree obtains its name from the large, ball-shaped fruits which, when ripe, contain a pulpy centre which is extremely foul smelling. A fine specimen can be seen opposite Queen's Royal College on the Port of Spain Savannah, and other good specimens can be seen in Georgetown (Guyana) and Trafalgar Square, Bridgetown, Barbados. The one in the photograph grows in Port of Spain.

Crepe Myrtle or Crape Myrtle (*Lagerstroemia indica*)
Other names   June Rose, Lilac of the South

This species is not a member of the true myrtle family, despite its name. It is a native of South East Asia and northern Australia but has now been introduced into many other parts of the world including the Caribbean. It produces paired, simple leaves which are dark green in colour. The flowers are produced in open terminal clusters. Floral colour varies, but the common colour in many Caribbean islands is light purple. Its timber is sometimes used commercially and has some medicinal use. The species grows particularly well in Trinidad (the specimen illustrated was photographed there) but it is found in other islands including Puerto Rico and Jamaica.

Family Leguminoseae

Divi-Livi (*Caesalpinia coriaria*)
Other names Livi-Divi, Divi Divi, Libi-Dibi

This tree grows to a height of about twenty five feet. It sometimes appears rather straggly and windblown. The shortish trunk often leans over and the crown becomes horizontal in appearance, a characteristic brought about by the prevailing wind. The leaves are fern-like and compound with small leaflets. The yellow flowers are small and produce a strong scent which attracts numerous insects for purposes of pollination. The fruits are pod-like and are a source of tannin. The specimen illustrated was photographed in Curacao where it is the national tree. This species is also found on Aruba and in botanical gardens in Trinidad and Dominica. Specimens can also be seen in Antigua and the Virgin Islands.

Family Apocynaceae

Frangipani (*Plumeria spp*)
Other names Pagoda Tree, Temple Tree

There are a number of varieties of Frangipani and the colour of the flowers varies; reddish orange, pink, yellow and white specimens are found. In the Caribbean, probably the two most common forms are the red (*P. rubra*) and the white (*P. alba*). The Frangipani is a small tree about fifteen feet in height with a multi-branched appearance. The leaves are large (about eight inches long), dark green, shiny and are oblong in shape. The leaves are shed in the dry season and flowering begins soon after the leaves have fallen. Each flower comprises five petals. The flowers produce a very sweet scent and, because of this, the tree has been planted extensively in temple gardens in eastern countries, hence its names 'Pagoda Tree' or 'Temple Tree'. The branches and leaves produce a white, milky sap which is poisonous. It is thought the white form is a native of the West Indies but the red variety originated in Central America. The specimens illustrated were photographed in Barbados.

Family Combretaceae

Indian Almond (*Terminalia catappa*)
Other names Almond Tree, Tropical Almond, West Indian Almond

This tree is a native of Malaysia and the East Indies but it has now been introduced into many parts of the tropics. Its spreading habit makes it ideal as a shade tree and, because it can withstand droughts, it is also common on sandy shores. It reaches a maximum height of about fifty feet, but specimens encountered in hotel grounds are usually much smaller. It produces branches in horizontal whorls. The leaves are alternate, each leaf being six to ten inches long. The texture is leathery and the appearance dark green and glossy on the upper surface. Leaves are shed from time to time and prior to detachment they turn bright red. The flowers are small, whitish in colour and grow in axillary spikes. The fruits are oval and greenish in colour. Each fruit is about two inches in length. The tree is found in many Caribbean islands and the visitor is likely to see it both in hotel grounds and on the beach. The specimen illustrated was photographed in Barbados.

Indian Banyan (*Ficus benghalensis*)

The Banyan belongs to the group of flowering plants which include other interesting forms such as the Edible Fig and Indian Rubber Tree. It originated in India, where it is considered sacred by Hindus. It is a large, spreading tree growing to a height of eighty feet or more. It produces large numbers of aerial roots which extend downwards to form secondary trunks when they reach the ground. The leaves are about six inches long, two to five inches broad and shiny and leathery in appearance. Each fig contains three kinds of flower; male, female and gall flowers, which are sterile female flowers containing the little wasps that pollinate the true female flowers. The 'fruit' is the fleshy receptable bearing the flowers on its internal surface. The tree often begins life as an epiphyte. Once established on its host tree it quickly grows and eventually 'strangles' the host, finally totally replacing it. The photograph was taken in Bermuda.

Family Zygophyllaceae

Lignum Vitae (*Guaiacum officinale*)
Other names Tree of Life

This tree grows to a height of between twenty and thirty feet. It produces large numbers of crooked branches and the rounded, dome-shaped form is very pronounced. Each leaf is composed of two or three pairs of stalk-less leaflets which are glossy and dark green in colour. The flowers are blue and are produced in axillary clusters of five to ten. The fruits are fleshy and orange in colour. The wood is one of the heaviest of commercial woods and it is highly resinous. It is used in the manufacture of functional parts such as pulley blocks, cogs and bearings. Gum guaiacum, collected from the bark, has been used in the treatment of arthritis and a decoction of the sap wood was used, until the development of more modern drugs, in the treatment of syphilis. The tree is common in parts of Jamaica (the flower is the national flower of Jamaica). It is also found in Trinidad and Tobago, St. Vincent, Dominica and Barbados and it is the national tree of the Bahamas. In Jamaica it blooms mainly in February but can flower at other times; in Barbados it flowers twice a year. It originated in South America.

Family Leguminoseae

Indian Laburnum (*Cassia fistula*)
Other names Golden Shower Tree, Pudding Pipe Tree, Shower of Gold

This tree is distributed widely throughout the tropics and is found in many Caribbean islands. It reaches a height of thirty feet or more and is often grown to provide shade. The trunk is slim and the upper branches tend to droop rather like its relative the Pink Cassia. The leaves are compound with two to eight pairs of leaflets, each three to four inches long. The flowers appear between April and July and, during this period, blossoms are produced in large numbers of yellow, hanging sprays. Each flower has five petals and the pistil and stamens are exposed. Each fertilised flower produces a long, dark brown fruit pod about two feet in length and pods often remain on the tree for a long time. The tree originated in tropical Asia and in India it is called the 'Pudding Pipe Tree'. The specimens illustrated were photographed in Trinidad.

Family Malvaceae

Mahoe (*Hibiscus elatus*)

This tree has a fairly short and sometimes twisted trunk which is crowned with a wide-spread and rounded top. The stalked-leaves are rounded with a heart-shaped base and each leaf is about six inches long. The foliage is rather a dull green and the upper surface of the leaves are smooth whilst the lower surface is rather hairy. A characteristic of the tree is the way many older leaves droop downwards from the stalk. The flowers are trumpet-shaped with yellow petals but in time the colour of the blossoms change to orange and even reddish brown. The tree bears flowers at various times throughout the year. The height of this species varies a great deal; most specimens seen on the roadside are of medium height but many cultivated specimens are smaller because of excessive pruning. It is not known where this species originated from but it is now widely distributed throughout the tropics.

Family Araucariaceae

Norfolk Island Pine (*Araucaria excelsa*)

This tree is grown as an ornamental specimen particularly in Barbados and Trinidad. It originated in Norfolk Island in the Pacific and it is said to have been discovered by Captain Cook. It is not a true pine. It reaches a height well over one hundred feet and grows very symmetrically, a feature which makes it popular in landscape gardening. The leaves arise in a spiral around the branch, no leaf ever arises opposite another. A close relative is the Monkey Puzzle (*A. imbricata*)

Family Leguminoseae

Pink Cassia (*Cassia javanica*)
Other names Apple Blossom Cassia, Pink Shower Tree

This tree grows to a height of about thirty feet and develops a spreading and arched canopy with the top branches tending to droop downwards. The tree originated on the island of Java but it has now been introduced widely throughout the tropics including many parts of the Caribbean. The leaves are compound, each with ten to thirty pairs of oblong-leaflets; each leaflet is about two inches long. The flowers are produced in clusters and the photograph shows the typical way in which they are borne. The colour varies from pale pink to rose pink; flowering occurs usually between April and June. After flowering, long fruit pods are produced which are dark brown in colour. The specimen in the photograph can be seen growing in the grounds of Sam Lord's Castle, Barbados.

Family Bignoniaceae

Pink Poui (*Tabebuia pentaphylla*)
Other names Pink Tecoma, Pink Trumpet, Trumpet Tree

Like its relative the Yellow Poui, this is one of the tallest forest forms reaching a height of seventy feet or more. It flowers in April and May and, in full bloom, it forms a very striking picture. The blossoms are produced when the leaves have dropped off. The flowers are trumpet-shaped and are produced in clusters. Some fine specimens can be seen on the Savannah, in front of the Queen's Royal College, Port of Spain. Although planted for its floral beauty it also functions as a shade tree among coffee and cocoa plantations. It is now distributed throughout a number of Caribbean islands. The specimens illustrated were photographed in Trinidad. The species originated in South America.

Family   Leguminoseae

Poinciana (*Delonix regia*)
Other names   Royal Poinciana, Flamboyant, Flame Tree

This tree, now widely distributed throughout the tropics, originated in Madagascar. It grows to a maximum height of about fifty feet and develops a flat, wide-spreading crown; sometimes the tree is wider than it is high. The leaves are compound. Each leaf is between one and two feet long, and it is divided into numerous leaflets, the effect being feathery and fern-like. The flowers are bright orange or red and sometimes scarlet. Each flower is about four inches in diameter and the blossoms erupt in huge terminal or axillary sprays. The time of flowering varies from one island to another; in Barbados the flowers are best seen between June and August, in Jamaica blossoms appear from May to July and in Trinidad fine specimens can be seen in flower in April. The fruits are produced as very large, flat pods about two feet in length and, during the dry season when the leaves are shed, the fruiting bodies are particularly conspicuous. The specimen illustrated was photographed in Trinidad.

Family Leguminoseae

Pride of Burma (*Amherstia nobilis*)
Other names Orchid Flower

This tree is included because of its general interest and beauty rather than its frequency. Indeed, it is a rare specimen. However, the beauty of its flowers, together with the fact that it is considered by many to be one of the most beautiful of flowering trees, make its inclusion essential. The tree was introduced into the botanical gardens in Port of Spain around the middle of the nineteenth century and since this date it has been taken to botanic gardens in Jamaica (Hope Gardens) and Dominica. In addition to the fine specimen in Port of Spain's botanic gardens another excellent specimen can be seen at Centano in Trinidad. The flowers bear a superficial resemblance to orchids, hence the common name. They hang down in large numbers and the pink, red and yellow colours give the blossoms a very striking appearance, particularly as they contrast strongly with the bright green foliage. The specimen illustrated was photographed in Trinidad.

Family Leguminoseae

Pride of India (*Peltophorum dubium*)

This tree is fairly common in the Caribbean region and is particularly well distributed on Barbados. It is a large tree often attaining a height of sixty or seventy feet. The crown has a characteristic rounded shape and the foliage is dark green. The leaves are compound and feathery. The tree flowers between March and July. The blossoms are yellowish-orange and are borne in erect, pyramid-shaped clusters about twelve inches long at the ends of the branches. After flowering, the fruits develop into flattened pods about five inches long and one inch wide. The tree originated in the Indo-Malaysian region. The specimen illustrated was photographed in Barbados.

Family Moraceae

Rubber (*Ficus elastica*)
Other names Indian Rubber Tree, Rubber Plant

This tree originated in India but it is now found throughout the tropics. In recent years it has become a favourite house plant in many temperate countries. It can grow to eighty feet or more in its native habitat but specimens seen in the Caribbean usually reach only about twenty feet. It is easily recognised by its large, leathery leaves each of which is enclosed in a reddish, pointed, protective sheath prior to its emergence. Like many members of the fig family, older trees produce aerial roots which eventually grow downwards and give the appearance of secondary trunks, a development taken to the extreme in the related Banyan Tree. The Indian Rubber Tree is now distributed widely in the Caribbean and is particularly common in Puerto Rico, the Virgin Islands, Barbados and Trinidad. Some fine mature specimens can be seen outside the Ministry of Education Building in Nassau, the Bahamas. The specimen illustrated was photographed in Barbados.

Silk Cotton (*Ceiba pentandra*)
Other names Cotton Tree, Kapok Tree

This large tree (often reaching more than one hundred feet in height) is a native of tropical America and the West Indies. It produces horizontal branches, usually beginning far up the trunk. The development of large buttress roots is a characteristic. The leaves are palmate with seven divisions; each leaf is about six inches in length. The flowers are whitish, two to three inches long and are produced in clusters. The time of flowering varies and in Barbados the blossoms appear in January and February. The fruits are pod-like and are filled with Kapok, a cotton-like material.

Family Malpighiaceae

Soufrière (*Spachea perforata*)

This tree has been included because it has a curiosity interest. It has been the official flower of St. Vincent since independence. Legend has it that 'the original plant was found on the slope of the Soufrière volcano before the 1812 eruption'. Recent discoveries, however, suggest that the tree originated in Guiana and was brought to St. Vincent by the curator Alexander Anderson, around 1785. This specimen can be seen in the Botanic Gardens in Kingstown. It does not set seed in the Gardens, but by means of vegetative propagation other plants have been obtained; one in another part of these Gardens and reportedly one other in the Botanic Gardens in Port of Spain, Trinidad.

Tamarind (*Tamarindus indica*)

The Tamarind originated in tropical Africa and was brought to the Caribbean in the early seventeenth century. It grows to a height of about fifty feet with a large crown of light green, feathery foliage. The leaves are compound, each leaf being formed of about fifteen pairs of leaflets. The tree flowers about the middle of year, the flowers being inconspicuous, small and light yellow in colour. The specimen illustrated was photographed in Barbados where this species is particularly common, especially because of its shade-providing qualities. The pod-like fruits, which are dark brown in colour, make a good purgative and can be used to make effective poultices. The pulp around the seeds is used to make a cooling drink. The wood is used in making local furniture.

Family Bignoniaceae

Yellow Elder (*Tecoma stans*)
Other names Yellow Trumpet, Yellow Cedar

This tree reaches a height of between twenty five and thirty feet. The foliage is darkish-green and the leaflets are long and pointed with serrated edges. The flowers are yellow and trumpet-shaped, occurring in groups of three to six. It is common in both the Bahamas and the U.S. Virgin Islands where it is the national flower. This choice results from the colour of the flower which represents the sunshine of the islands and the fact that the tree needs no care to flourish thus representing the stout qualities of the Bahamian people. This specimen was photographed in the Bahamas.

Family Bignoniaceae

Yellow Poui (*Tebebuia serratifolia*)
Other names Apamata, Gold Tree

This tree originated in central and northern South America and is now found in several Caribbean islands including Trinidad and Barbados. It grows to a height of seventy or eighty feet and, because of its dense resinous wood, it is used extensively in building and construction; it is very resistant to termites. Each leaf is palmately compound and comprises five to seven leaflets which are silvery green in colour. The leaves are shed early in the dry season (January to February) and new foliage is not produced for three or four months. Flowering takes place in April and the blossoms last for only a few days. Each flower is yellow in colour and the corolla is trumpet-shaped. Flowers are produced in clusters. The specimen illustrated was photographed in Trinidad where particularly fine specimens are found.

2 *Fruit Trees*

Banana (*Musa spp.*)

Family Sapindaceae

Akee (*Blighia sapida*)
Other names Ackee, Akee Akee, Vegetable Brain

This tree originated in West Africa and is said to have been introduced into Jamaica by Captain Bligh (commander of H.M.S. *Bounty*) in 1778. It is now the national fruit of Jamaica. The tree reaches a height of about thirty feet. The leaves are compound, comprising four or five pairs of leaflets. The flowers are produced in axillary racemes and each blossom is small, greenish white in colour with a pleasant fragrance. The fruits develop thick, reddish-orange skins which enclose shiny, black seeds (three per fruit body). At the base of the seeds is a fleshy, whitish-coloured structure called the aril. This is the only edible part of the fruit. However, it can be cooked and eaten safely only when ripe. Unripened arils, or those over-ripe, are poisonous and 'Jamaica poisoning' is the term given to the condition resulting in death which is caused by eating arils at the wrong stage of development. Although found in other Caribbean islands, it is most common in Jamaica where a popular dish is 'salt fish and akee'.

Family Lauraceae

Avocado (*Persea americana*)
Other names Alligator Pear, Pear

This is a medium sized tree attaining a height of about thirty feet. The foliage is dark green and shiny, each leaf being about six inches in length and three inches wide. The flowers are inconspicuous and light green in colour; they are borne in clusters. The fruit develops into a thick, fleshy structure with a hard stone in the centre. The size and shape of the fruit varies; some are round others eliptical and the common form is pear-shaped. The flesh is soft when ripe and light yellowish-green in colour. It is eaten both in salads and as an entree to main courses and is popular not only in the tropics but also in temperate countries.

Family Musaceae

Banana (*Musa spp*)

The most commonly eaten raw banana is the species *Musa sapientum*. A coarser variety often called 'plantain' (*Musa paradisiaca*) is not eaten raw but is prepared by boiling or frying. Botanically, a banana tree is a perennial herb which grows to a height of twenty to thirty feet, depending on the species. Bananas originated in the Indo-Malaysian region but they are now distributed widely throughout the tropics. The leaves are from five to twelve feet long and a foot or so wide. They grow in a whorl-like fashion at the top of the 'stalk', the latter being made up of overlapping leaf bases. The clusters of flowers are covered with reddish-purple bracts and the complete inflorescence hangs down on a long stalk. Only the first group of flowers develop into fruit. Flowering and fruiting occur throughout the year but each stem bears only one batch of fruit. After producing this fruit it dies. New plants are replaced by suckers which develop from the root stock.

Family Moraceae

Breadfruit (*Artocarpus communis*)

This tree attains a height of sixty feet or more but smaller specimens are commonly seen. It originated in the South Pacific and was first brought from Tahiti to the Caribbean by Captain Bligh in the ship *Providence* in 1793. It was thought the fruit would provide food for slaves on sugar planations and, since the early days of slavery, the tree has spread throughout the Caribbean. The leaves grow to three feet in length and are deeply lobed. The upper surface is dark green and smooth whereas the lower is paler with distinct veins. The male flowers are in yellow catkins about sixteen inches long. The female flowers form round and prickly clusters. The mature fruits are spherical and about eight inches in diameter. They are greenish-yellow with a rough skin. The tree is propagated by cuttings since it seldom produces seeds. Another variety of *Artocarpus* produces a 'seeded' fruit which is round with spiny projections and is known as the 'Breadnut Tree'. The fruit is eaten either boiled, roasted or baked and has a slight nutty flavour.

Family Anacardiaceae

Cashew (*Anacardium occidentale*)

This tree grows to a height of between twenty and forty feet. The leaves arise alternately, each being about six inches in length, yellowish-green in colour and with a leathery texture. The flowers are pale yellow in colour. The most interesting feature is the strange fruit called the Cashew Apple. This is a fleshy structure which is reddish in colour and shaped rather like a pear. The real fruit is a nut which is borne at the end of the Cashew Apple. It is the kernel of the nut which is used commercially. The Cashew probably originated in South America and the West Indies. The oily 'shell-liquid' is poisonous. The 'shell liquid' is used in electrical insulation in aircraft, but its poisonous qualities have been known to affect maintenance men handling such insulated cables.

Family Sterculiaceae

Cocoa (*Theobroma cacao*)
Other names Chocolate Tree

This tree originated in Central and South America but has now become distributed in many parts of the tropics including the Caribbean. The Aztecs cultivated the tree before the Europeans reached tropical America and Christopher Columbus took cocoa beans back to Spain in 1502. Various recipes using the beans were developed in Europe, but it was not until the middle of the nineteenth century that chocolate appeared as a confection. The Spanish explorers introduced the tree to Trinidad in 1625 and plantations were quickly developed. Later, a second variety arrived and thus began the process of hybridization. Trees are now found in other parts of the Caribbean and visitors to Tobago and Grenada will find them a common feature of the landscape.

47

Family Moraceae

Jackfruit (*Artocarpus heterophyllus*)
Other names Jak Fruit

This tree originated in the Indo-Malaysian region but it is now found in many tropical regions. It is a member of the fig family and is related to the Breadfruit Tree. It reaches a height of fifty feet or more and has a spreading habit. The leaves are variable in shape and can be obovate, narrow or oblong; each leaf is about six inches long. The small flowers are either male or female, and male and female blossoms are often found on the same branch. Their colour varies from yellowish to green. The green fruits vary in shape and ripen during the rainy season between June and September. They grow to eighteen inches in length and attain a weight of more than forty pounds. Fruits can be eaten raw or cooked but they are less popular than Breadfruits. The seeds of the fruit are often roasted and eaten in a similar way to chestnuts. A yellow dye is sometimes extracted from the wood and this is used for dyeing clothes, particularly in India and the Far East.

Mango (*Mangifera indica*)

This tree originated in tropical Asia, but has now become established throughout the tropics. It attains a height of fifty feet and develops a rounded crown, usually above a short trunk. Trees grown on plantations (for commercial purposes) are often shorter in height. The leaves are six to ten inches in length, leathery and with a shiny surface. The small flowers are greenish-white in colour and grow in terminal clusters, each about eight inches in length. Flowering usually occurs in the dry season. Each fruit is kidney-shaped, about five inches long and hangs from a long stalk. The fruit is very popular and is eaten raw or made into chutneys and preserves. Fruits usually ripen in the wet season. The photographs were taken in Barbados.

Family Myristicaceae

Nutmeg (*Myristica fragrans*)

This tree originated in the East Indies. It can reach a height of sixty feet and is found in a number of islands including Trinidad, Dominica and Grenada. This latter island annually exports about two thousand tons of nutmeg to the United States. The leaves are simple, oily and evergreen. The flowers are inconspicuous with reduced parts. The fruit looks like a small peach and inside is found the seed covered by a red layer called an aril. When dried, the aril is known as the spice mace. The outer pulp of the fruit is fermented to form a 'brandy-type' drink with a characteristic bouquet and taste. The seed is the nutmeg of commerce. The photographs are of a specimen in the botanic gardens in St. Vincent. Some particularly good specimens can be seen in Welchman Hall Gully in Barbados.

Family Caricaceae

Pawpaw (*Carica papaya*)

This is a quick growing tree which may reach a height of twenty feet. Rarely does the tree branch, thus the trunk is crowned with a mass of leaves at the top. The stem is hollow and not woody. The leaves are large, palmately shaped and each has six lobes or more. Usually a tree bears only one sexual form of flower and only female trees produce fruits after fertilisation of their flowers. The fruits vary in shape and may be elongated or round and weights of ten pounds are not uncommon for a single specimen. The flesh of the fruit is yellowish-orange when ripe and is eaten raw, often as a breakfast dish with a slice of lime. The fruit contains the enzyme papain, a proteolytic enzyme, and this is used commercially for tenderising meat. Local inhabitants in many islands wrap meat in pawpaw leaves prior to cooking in order to make the meat more tender. The tree is a native of the West Indies and tropical America. In some parts of the world it is commonly known as Papaya.

Family Sapotaceae

Sapodilla (*Manilkara zapota*)
Other names Naseberry

This tree is a native of the West Indies and Central America. It is fairly slow growing, but eventually it will reach a height of fifty feet or more. The leaves are produced alternately and are leathery in texture. Each leaf is about four inches long with a shiny, dark green surface. The flowers are small and white. The fruit is round in shape, about two inches in diameter and has a reddish-brown skin. The pulp is eaten raw and is considered to have a pleasant flavour. Chicle gum is extracted from the sap of the trunk and this is used in the manufacture of chewing gum. Each tree should be tapped only once in every six years, but, in practice, this rule is not always followed with the result that many trees die, usually from disease.

Family Annonaceae

Soursop (*Annona muricata*)

This is a fast growing tree which reaches a height of about thirty feet. The leaves are produced alternately, each being about four inches in length, and shiny on the upper surface. The flowers are yellowish-green in colour and are borne sometimes singly and sometimes in groups. The fruit is large and a single specimen may weigh as much as six pounds. The skin is covered in spines clearly seen in the photograph. This tree comes from tropical America but is found in many parts of the Caribbean where its fruit is particularly popular, especially when sieved and served as 'Soursop Ice Cream'.

3 Coast Trees

Sea Grape (*Coccoloba uvifera*)

Family   Casuarinaceae

Casuarina (*Cassuarina equisetifolia*)
Other names   Willow, Whistling Pine, Australian Pine, Beefwood,
                She Oak

This is a fast growing tree which reaches a height of seventy feet or more. It produces long, drooping, feathery branches. Its fast growing habit makes it useful as a hedge, but it requires careful clipping. The branches bear small, brown scale-like structures. The male flowers form thin spikes at the tips of branches; the female flowers form cone-like structures. This tree originated in Australia and the Pacific region, but it has now been introduced into many parts of the tropics. It certainly arrived in Jamaica towards the end of the eighteenth century. It has been used extensively in preventing movement of sand because of its many root structures which serve to bind the substrate. It is a common feature of many Caribbean coastal areas. The specimens illustrated were photographed in Barbados.

Family Euphorbiaceae

Manchineel (*Hippomane mancinella*)

This tree is a native of the coasts of Central America and the Caribbean. It reaches a height of between twenty and forty feet and develops a wide spreading crown. The leaves are two to four inches long on long stalks. The flowers are either male or female, both types being borne on the same tree. They are green and inconspicuous. The green, roundish fruits are extremely poisonous. Many hotels display signs warning of the dangers of this tree. The tree produces a milky sap which is a severe irritant to both skin and eyes, and bad cases of blistering have been reported from tourists handling leaves of this species. The specimen was photographed in the grounds of Sam Lord's Castle in Barbados.

Family Boraginaceae

Cordia (*Cordia sebestena*)
Other names Scarlet Cordia, Geranium Tree

This tree flourishes in dry soils and is tolerant of salt conditions. It is found throughout the Caribbean being particularly common on Barbados. It reaches a height of about twenty five feet and tends to flower throughout the year. The oval leaves are three to eight inches long, with a dark green, rough upper surface. The reddish-orange flowers are borne in clusters six to eight inches across. The petals are 'papery' in appearance and texture and are frilled at the edges. The fruits are plum-like. This tree is a native of the Caribbean. The specimen in the photograph is to be found in the grounds of the Paradise Beach Hotel in Barbados.

Family Polygonaceae

Sea Grape (*Coccoloba uvifera*)

This species varies in habit depending upon the environment in which it grows. On exposed sea shores it grows as a sprawling shrub but in more sheltered areas it grows as a tree, reaching a height of about fifty feet. It is very characteristic of many Caribbean beaches and is a species which the tourist will readily see. The leaves have a characteristic shape each one being rounded and up to eight inches across. They are smooth and leathery with a shiny surface and reddish veins. The male and female flowers occur on different trees and the female flowers, after fertilisation, develop into clusters of grape-like fruits which become purple in colour. The fruits are edible but rather sour. However, they can be made into a pleasant tasting preserve. This species is a native of the Caribbean region and coastal Central America but it has now been introduced into many tropical areas. Some historians suggest this was the first plant seen by Columbus when he came to the Caribbean region in the fifteenth century.

4 Palms and Palm-Like Trees

Latania loddigesii

Cabbage Palm (*Roystonea oleracea*)

This is one of the tallest of the palm family and specimens may reach up to one hundred and thirty feet in height. The trunk is slim apart from a slight swelling at the base, and, for most of its length, it rarely exceeds twenty inches in diameter. The leaves appear in a crown at the top of the trunk, each leaf being about fifteen feet long and comprising a large number of pointed leaflets. Each leaf has a leaf base in the form of a sheath which is attached to the trunk for several feet. The flowers are formed in the base of the green leaf sheaths and they grow in clusters. The fruits are small, hard and nut-like and when ripe appear dark purplish-red. The terminal bud is considered a delicacy and is the main ingredient for 'millionaires salad'. It can be eaten raw or cooked. This species of palm is often planted in rows and the visitor to Barbados will see a fine avenue at Codrington College; the photograph illustrates this particular avenue. This species is a native of the Caribbean, being particularly common in Barbados, Trinidad and the Windward Islands.

Family Palmae

Coconut Palm (*Cocos nucifera*)
Other names Coco Palm, Coconut Tree

This palm is widely dispersed throughout the tropics. Tall specimens may reach a height of eighty feet or more. The trunk is often bent and is usually thickened at the base. The leaves arise in a crown at the top, each leaf being about fifteen feet in length with many leaflets. The leaves are fibrous in texture. The flowers grow among the leaves and are yellowish-white in colour. The fruits are large rounded structures covered with smooth, thick husks. The 'nut' is found inside and the layer between the fruit outer wall and the shell of the 'nut' is formed of a tough, fibrous material which is used commercially. The kernel of the 'nut' is widely eaten and the central cavity of the mature fruit is filled with a liquid which is refeshing to drink. The leaves are used for thatching roofs and, in many islands, coconut oil is extracted from the fruit and used in cooking. The dried fruit is the 'copra' of commerce.

Family Cycadaceae

Cycad (*Cycas spp*)

The Cycads are not members of the Palm family, despite their appearance. They are a primitive group of plants which have changed little in appearance over the last two hundred million years. Their fossil remains are almost identical with living specimens and hence such plants are commonly referred to as 'living fossils'. The tree is columnar and has an erect cylindrical stem which can grow to a height of between ten and thirty feet. It does, however, grow very slowly and will only reach its maximum height after many centuries. The stem is surmounted with a crown of large, fern-like leaves which are dark green in colour. A new crown of leaves is produced annually in some species and biennially in others, and the leaves of each crown may persist for several years. The tree is cone bearing. Each tree bears only one kind of cone, either seed cones or pollen cones. The Cycads are grown for ornamental purposes on many Caribbean islands and they can be found in both hotel grounds and private gardens.

Family Palmae

Royal Palm (*Roystonea regia*)
Other names Mountain Cabbage

This tree originated in Cuba but is now widely distributed throughout the Caribbean. It frequently grows to a height of sixty feet and some specimens may reach nearly one hundred feet. Its greyish trunk grows very erect but in many specimens a swelling occurs about half way up. The huge leaves arise from the top, each leaf being about fifteen feet in length with many three-feet long leaflets. The flowers arise in the leaf bases and develop in panicles. Many fruits are formed, each one being oval in shape and purple in colour. The specimens in the photograph are to be found bordering the botanic gardens in Port of Spain, Trinidad.

Traveller's Tree (*Ravenala madagascariensis*)

Other names   Traveller's Palm

This tree resembles a member of the palm family but in fact it belongs to the group of plants which includes the bananas. It derives its name from the fact that the hollow leaf stalks form receptacles at their bases where water can accumulate after rain, and thus a ready supply of liquid refreshment is always available. The tree originated in the island of Madagascar but is now distributed widely throughout the tropics. It is particularly attractive because its leaves grow mainly in one plane (the vertical one) and, thus, mature specimens look like giant green fans. The photograph was taken in the botanic gardens in St. Vincent.

Family Pandanaceae

Screw Pine (*Pandanus utilis*)
Other names Screw Palm

This species is not a palm, despite its appearance, and is a shrub rather than a tree, although it often attains tree-like proportions. It originated in the Pacific region where it is used to provide materials for thatching, basket weaving, mat making and construction work. In the Caribbean some parts of the vegetation are used to make brushes. The appearance of this species is unusual; it branches at ground level and the short stems quickly become supported by 'stilt roots' which themselves become quite thick. The leaves appear at the ends of the branches of the trunk. They develop in clusters, each leaf being about five feet in length and three inches in width. The margins are serrated. The common name for this species is because the leaves arise in a spiral formation resembling a screw. The specimen illustrated was photographed in St. Vincent.

Visitor's check list

Date	Name of tree	Place where seen	Additional notes

Visitor's check list

Date	Name of tree	Place where seen	Additional notes